SO YOU WANT TO
Volunteer

plan and journal your adventure

Heidi van 't Riet

LE NOBLE

Le Noble Publishing

Published by Le Noble Publishing 2016
First edition; First Printing

Design and writing © 2016 Heidi van 't Riet

Cover design by Julia Kuris

ISBN 978-0-9967769-0-5

Dedication

This book is dedicated to the people who made our volunteering journey one of the most unique and rewarding experiences of our lives.

Introduction

Volunteer work can be incredibly rewarding. Many people talk about it as being life-changing. Under any circumstance, it is an experience you will never forget.

Volunteering is also work. When you undertake a project - be it several weeks or months - you commit to doing a job in a host location, contributing to your fullest. You will get out of the experience what you put in, and, if all goes well, a lot more.

I spent 8 months traveling with my family around the world. We volunteered in 5 different countries. We mainly taught English, though we are not trained as teachers. My children, who were 11 and 13 at the time, taught with us. They loved working with kids across the globe; soccer and friendship bracelets overcame any language barrier! Each experience taught us deeply about the cultures we visited, the people we met and, ultimately, ourselves.

You have taken a step into a wonderful adventure by buying this book. I hope that your volunteer work will be as enriching, satisfying and fun as ours!

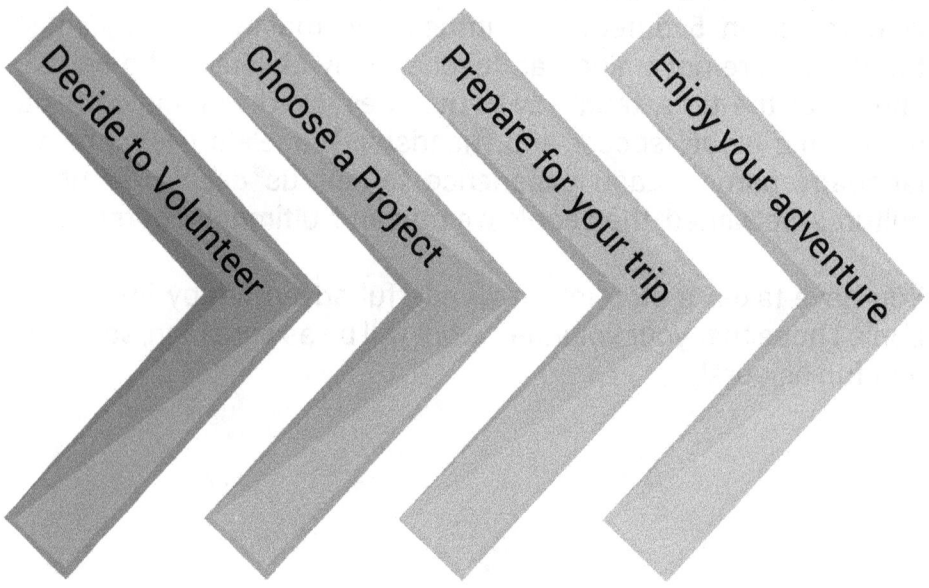

How to use this book

Congratulations on making the decision to volunteer! Dedicating your time and energy to a community that needs your help is a noble commitment. In return, you will learn a lot about yourself and the world we live in.

This book is intended as a place to keep all of your research together and to journal about your adventure. As we prepared for our trip, we found there was a vast amount of information we needed to sort through. We wanted to make sure we were well prepared, yet we found no simple way to keep everything organized. This book is based on our experiences. It is intended to be a workbook to keep all of your planning details together and easily accessible. The journal allows you to capture your thoughts through planning and travel, making it an invaluable keepsake of your journey.

The book is broken into sections. The first part of the book helps you explore your interests and motivation. You can answer questions about why and how you want to volunteer. Take the time to reflect and write this down. Knowing why you are volunteering will help guide your decisions later. Next, the focus is on project selection. The third section has a series of practical checklists to organize your travel. Finally, there is a journal where you can record your experiences and adventures.

There are a lot of internet resources and books available to answer questions, from which projects you can do to which backpack is best for a 6-month trip. Make use of these resources. Inform yourself and you will enjoy your trip much more. As a starting point, you can find links and ideas on our website www.PlanToVolunteer.com.

As you prepare, keep in mind that doing your homework and planning will make your trip smoother and less stressful. Expect and enjoy that some things will need to be adjusted and changed as you go along. Be flexible, have a positive mindset and don't hesitate to ask for help when you need it!

Enjoy your journey!

Pull out your pens and pencils

This book is meant to be written in, drawn in and scribbled on. Use it as a notepad and a guide, a memoir and a keepsake.

For more resources and information, please visit:

www.PlanToVolunteer.com

Table of Contents

Get Ready
Choosing Your Volunteer Project

As you grow older, you will discover that you have two hands, one for helping yourself, the other for helping others.

- Audrey Hepburn

Where to start?

The greatest volunteering experiences come from finding a match between you and a project. How do you do that? Before leaping into a lot of research and spending hours on the internet, consider why you decided to volunteer. What are you hoping to get out of your project and your adventure? Take some time to dream a little...

Why am I volunteering?

_____

_____

_____

_____

_____

_____

_____

_____

What goal do I want to achieve? (e.g., learn a language, get professional experience, learn another culture, travel differently)

_____

_____

_____

_____

_____

_____

_____

How much time do I have?

_____

_____

_____

How much time will I spend volunteering (and traveling)?

_____

_____

_____

When do I plan to have this adventure?

_____

_____

_____

_____

_____

Where do I want to go? What are the top locations to consider?

_____

_____

_____

_____

_____

_____

What do I hope to get out of my project?

_____

_____

_____

_____

_____

_____

_____

What skills or knowledge can I offer?

_____

_____

_____

_____

What kind of project interests me (conservation, teaching, etc.)?

_____

_____

_____

_____

_____

_____

Do what you can to show you care about other people, and you will make our world a better place.

-Rosalynn Carter

Identifying Agencies and Projects

There are thousands of volunteer projects available in every corner of the world. Identifying a project can feel like an overwhelming task when you start your research. By structuring your search, you can find a great project quickly. You can look for projects in one of two ways:

1. Use a volunteer agency to help you select a project. The agency will make the arrangements through their network of volunteering organizations, often across countries. They ensure that you are supported and prepared before you go and while you are working.

2. Organize a project yourself. You contact a local agency or a project and make arrangements directly with them.

Organizing a project on your own means contacting a local organization and asking if you can work with them. This may be slightly less expensive in terms of the cost of the project, but you will need to invest time to define your work scope, find accommodation, etc. If you are an experienced volunteer/traveler, you may have your own network to leverage. If not, you may want to consider an agency to help you with these arrangements.

When you **work via an agency**, the agency handles a lot of the legwork. You can take advantage of their experience and network to find a project that fits your interests best. They will make sure that you have accommodation, a defined project and connect you with the local staff to help you with logistics and support. It is advisable that you research the agencies carefully to make sure they have a good reputation/ratings for delivering the services they promise.

On the next pages, you can record your research into agencies. You may contact several and recording information about each can help in your assessment. After that, you will find pages to explore specific projects, directly or via an agency. Note: you may find that you do your project research and your agency research in parallel. That is fine, this is not necessarily a linear process. You will learn as you go.

Volunteer Agency Information

Name _____

Website _____

Contact _____

Application fees_____

Specialties _____

_____

_____

Locations _____

_____

_____

_____

What is my money used for? _____

_____

_____

Notes _____

_____

_____

_____

_____

_____

Feedback/Ratings from previous volunteers

_____

_____

_____

_____

_____

_____

Benefits _____

_____

_____

_____

_____

_____

Concerns _____

_____

_____

_____

_____

_____

Volunteer Agency Information

Name _____

Website _____

Contact _____

Application fees_____

Specialties _____

_____

_____

Locations _____

_____

_____

_____

What is my money used for? _____

_____

_____

Notes _____

_____

_____

_____

_____

_____

Feedback/Ratings from previous volunteers

_____

_____

_____

_____

_____

_____

_____

Benefits _____

_____

_____

_____

_____

_____

Concerns _____

_____

_____

_____

_____

_____

Volunteer Agency Information

Name _____

Website _____

Contact _____

Application fees_____

Specialties _____

_____

_____

Locations _____

_____

_____

_____

What is my money used for? _____

_____

_____

Notes _____

_____

_____

_____

_____

_____

_____

Feedback/Ratings from previous volunteers

_____

_____

_____

_____

_____

_____

Benefits _____

_____

_____

_____

_____

Concerns _____

_____

_____

_____

_____

_____

Volunteer Agency Information

Name _____

Website _____

Contact _____

Application fees_____

Specialties _____

_____

_____

Locations _____

_____

_____

What is my money used for? _____

_____

_____

Notes _____

_____

_____

_____

_____

Feedback/Ratings from previous volunteers

_____

_____

_____

_____

_____

_____

Benefits _____

_____

_____

_____

_____

Concerns _____

_____

_____

_____

_____

_____

Volunteer Agency Information

Name _____

Website _____

Contact _____

Application fees_____

Specialties _____

_____

_____

Locations _____

_____

_____

_____

What is my money used for? _____

_____

_____

Notes _____

_____

_____

_____

_____

_____

Feedback/Ratings from previous volunteers

_____

_____

_____

_____

_____

_____

Benefits _____

_____

_____

_____

_____

Concerns _____

_____

_____

_____

_____

_____

Volunteer Agency Information

Name _____

Website _____

Contact _____

Application fees_____

Specialties _____

_____

_____

Locations _____

_____

_____

_____

What is my money used for? _____

_____

_____

Notes _____

_____

_____

_____

_____

_____

Feedback/Ratings from previous volunteers

_____

_____

_____

_____

_____

_____

Benefits _____

_____

_____

_____

_____

_____

Concerns _____

_____

_____

_____

_____

_____

I am only one, but I am one. I cannot do everything, but I can do something. And I will not let what I cannot do interfere with what I can do.

- Edward Everett Hale

Selecting a Project

Choosing a project is an exciting step in the preparation.

Review what you wrote about what you would like to get out of your project. Research the locations you want to visit and the kinds of projects available there. As you investigate the projects, take notes and investigate the ones you think best fit your interests, skills and budget. At the same time, be sure to reflect if the project is useful in the context of the local community.

Having explored options, what types of projects interest me most?

_____

_____

_____

_____

_____

What are my key factors in choosing a project (location, type of work, agency, etc.)?

_____

_____

_____

_____

Where can I do this kind of work?

_____

_____

_____

_____

Volunteer Project Information

Agency   _____

Project   _____

Purpose   _____

Cost   _____

_____

Accommodation _____

_____

What have previous volunteers said? _____

_____

_____

_____

Benefits   _____

_____

_____

Concerns   _____

_____

_____

What is my money used for? _____

_____

_____

Volunteer Project Information

Agency   _____

Project   _____

Purpose   _____

Cost   _____

_____

Accommodation _____

_____

What have previous volunteers said? _____

_____

_____

_____

Benefits   _____

_____

_____

Concerns   _____

_____

_____

What is my money used for? _____

_____

_____

Volunteer Project Information

Agency _____

Project _____

Purpose _____

Cost _____

_____

Accommodation _____

_____

What have previous volunteers said? _____

_____

_____

_____

Benefits _____

_____

_____

Concerns _____

_____

_____

What is my money used for? _____

_____

_____

Volunteer Project Information

Agency _____

Project _____

Purpose _____

Cost _____

_____

Accommodation _____

_____

What have previous volunteers said? _____

_____

_____

_____

Benefits _____

_____

_____

Concerns _____

_____

_____

What is my money used for? _____

_____

_____

Volunteer Project Information

Agency _____

Project _____

Purpose _____

Cost _____

_____

Accommodation _____

_____

What have previous volunteers said? _____

_____

_____

_____

Benefits _____

_____

_____

Concerns _____

_____

_____

What is my money used for? _____

_____

_____

Volunteer Project Information

Agency   _____

Project   _____

Purpose   _____

Cost   _____

_____

Accommodation _____

_____

What have previous volunteers said? _____

_____

_____

_____

Benefits   _____

_____

_____

Concerns   _____

_____

_____

What is my money used for? _____

_____

_____

Volunteer Project Information

Agency _____

Project _____

Purpose _____

Cost _____

_____

Accommodation _____

_____

What have previous volunteers said? _____

_____

_____

_____

Benefits _____

_____

_____

Concerns _____

_____

_____

What is my money used for? _____

_____

_____

Volunteer Project Information

Agency _____

Project _____

Purpose _____

Cost _____

_____

Accommodation _____

_____

What have previous volunteers said? _____

_____

_____

_____

Benefits _____

_____

_____

Concerns _____

_____

_____

What is my money used for? _____

_____

_____

Volunteer Project Information

Agency _____

Project _____

Purpose _____

Cost _____

_____

Accommodation _____

_____

What have previous volunteers said? _____

_____

_____

_____

Benefits _____

_____

_____

Concerns _____

_____

_____

What is my money used for? _____

_____

_____

Volunteer Project Information

Agency _____

Project _____

Purpose _____

Cost _____

_____

Accommodation _____

_____

What have previous volunteers said? _____

_____

_____

_____

Benefits _____

_____

_____

Concerns _____

_____

_____

What is my money used for? _____

_____

_____

Help one another; there's no time like the present and no present like the time.

- James Durst

Budgeting

Volunteering abroad will cost money. You will generally need to pay for your transportation, accommodation, food and insurance while you are working on your project as well as any travel before or after your project.

What is the budget for your trip? You need to research the cost of transportation, accommodation and touring to determine an appropriate budget. Don't forget to include costs you incur **before** you leave home like visits to the doctor, buying gear and insurance.

Later in the book, there is a section dedicated to funding and tracking the money you need for your trip.

You will need to re-visit your budget regularly as you learn more about your host location, project and travel. Plan to have some extra money in case something unexpected comes up.

Item	Estimated Cost
Flights	
Visa	
Insurance	
Clothing	
Vaccinations	
Language lessons	
Travel/tours	
Local transportation	

Budget

Item	Estimated Cost

Budget

Item	Estimated Cost

Budget Notes

Get Set
Making your plans

Basics
Learn about the location
Learn some new words
Preparing for travel
Get ready for your volunteer work
Funding
Packing lists

The world is hugged by the faithful arms of volunteers.

- Terri Guillemets

Travel Basics

Now that you have a project identified, it is time to start getting ready for your trip. There are some primary logistics to take care of, such as booking your flights. You also need to investigate what you should take with you. This is a great time to start learning a little more about where you are going. The more you research, the more you will learn, observe and appreciate your travel.

Where do I need to be?

_____

_____

_____

When do I need to arrive at my volunteer location?

_____

_____

_____

Where do I want to travel before/after my project?

_____

_____

_____

_____

_____

_____

_____

Unselfish and noble actions are the most radiant pages in the biography of souls.

- David Thomas

Learn about the location

Learning a little about your host community will make it more comfortable for you when you arrive. A lot of information can be found online. Your project coordinator will also be able to help answer many of your questions. Awareness of local culture and customs can help you hit the ground running and deal with any culture shock. Be sure to investigate local climate and living conditions so you have appropriate clothing and gear.

Time zone and time difference to home _____

Climate & Season _____

_____

_____

_____

_____

What are local sites to visit?

_____

_____

_____

_____

_____

Safety & Security _____

_____

_____

_____

What are some of the local customs?

_____

_____

_____

_____

_____

When are important local holidays? How are they celebrated?

_____

_____

_____

_____

_____

What are some key historical events of the country/region?

_____

_____

_____

_____

_____

_____

What is typical housing?

_____

_____

_____

_____

_____

_____

What kind of schooling do children receive?

_____

_____

_____

_____

_____

What is the typical diet? What are key crops and foods?

_____

_____

_____

_____

_____

_____

Learn some new words

Speaking a few words in the local language is a great way to start making connections with the people in your host community. They will love helping you learn their language. There are lots of internet resources and books to help you learn your first phrases.

Hello _____

My name is _____

Please _____

Thank you _____

Can you please help me? _____

I'm sorry I don't speak _____

Do you speak _____ _____

Numbers 1-10 _____

_____ _____

_____ _____

_____ _____

_____ _____

_____ _____

_____ _____

_____ _____

_____ _____

Act as if what you do makes a difference.
It does.

- William James

Preparing for Travel

Now that you know where you are going and when, you can start to organize the logistics of your travel.

There are quite a lot of things to arrange such as:

- Flights
- Ground Transportation
- Accommodation
- Travel Insurance
- Medical Preparation
- Passports & Visas
- Electricity & Connectivity
- Gear

On the following pages, you can record information about each of these subjects so it is always easy to find and track.

When planning travel, check different options to find a solution that is most cost effective and efficient for you. There are usually several different ways of arriving at any location and you may find differences in prices by changing your flight timings and the arrival or destination airports.

Your volunteer coordinator may be able to help you identify some of these options, though you will need to select and make the final arrangements yourself.

At this point, you should also think about how long and where you want to travel before and/or after your project. This helps to ensure your flight tickets are booked correctly and avoid any change fees. That said, leave yourself some flexibility since you will certainly learn a lot from locals and other volunteers about interesting things to see and do in your host location.

After you have gotten information about general costs, don't forget to ***update your budget***.

Flight Options

Date _____

Route _____

Timings _____

Website/Source_____

Cost [   ]

Date _____

Route _____

Timings _____

Website/Source_____

Cost [   ]

Date _____

Route _____

Timings _____

Website/Source_____

Cost [   ]

Flight Options

Date _____

Route _____

Timings _____

Website/Source_____

Cost [_____]

Date _____

Route _____

Timings _____

Website/Source_____

Cost [_____]

Date _____

Route _____

Timings _____

Website/Source_____

Cost [_____]

Ground Transportation

Type _____

From-To _____

Website/Source _____

Notes _____

Cost [_____]

Type _____

From-To _____

Website/Source _____

Notes _____

Cost [_____]

Type _____

From-To _____

Website/Source _____

Notes _____

Cost [_____]

Ground Transportation

Type   _____

From-To   _____

Website/Source_____

Notes   _____

Cost [   ]

Type   _____

From-To   _____

Website/Source_____

Notes   _____

Cost [   ]

Type   _____

From-To   _____

Website/Source_____

Notes   _____

Cost [   ]

Accommodation

Location _____

Dates _____

Website/Source_____

Notes _____

Cost [   ]

Location _____

Dates _____

Website/Source_____

Notes _____

Cost [   ]

Location _____

Dates _____

Website/Source_____

Notes _____

Cost [   ]

Accommodation

Location   _____

Dates   _____

Website/Source _____

Notes   _____

Cost   [   ]

===

Location   _____

Dates   _____

Website/Source _____

Notes   _____

Cost   [   ]

===

Location   _____

Dates   _____

Website/Source _____

Notes   _____

Cost   [   ]

===

Things to do and see

Things to do and see

Travel Insurance/Medical Insurance

Travel insurance is usually required when you do a volunteer project. Check with your volunteer agency or coordinator for additional information about the kind of insurance needed for your project.

What kind of coverage do I need?

_____

_____

Will I keep my insurance at home? _____

Company _____

Cost _____

Coverage _____

_____

_____

Company _____

Cost _____

Coverage _____

_____

_____

Company _____

Cost _____

Coverage _____

_____

_____

Vaccinations and Malaria

Before you travel abroad, it is important to check if you need any vaccinations or malaria protection. Ask your doctor about medication you should carry in your first aid kit.

What vaccinations do I need before departure?

_____

_____

_____

How long before my trip do I need the vaccinations?

_____

_____

_____

Is there any malaria risk where I am going?

_____

_____

What are the options for malaria protection?

_____

_____

_____

What should I carry in my first aid kit?

_____

_____

_____

Passports and Visas

Do you have a passport? Is it up to date? For many countries, you'll need up to 6 months validity after you arrive. If you don't have a passport, apply for one early.

Do I need to get/renew my passport? How do I do that?

_____

_____

_____

What kind of visa will I need to get for my host country?

_____

_____

_____

How do I get the visa for the host country?

_____

_____

_____

How long does a visa last? Can it be extended?

_____

_____

Do I need visas for other countries I plan to visit?

_____

_____

_____

Electricity and Connectivity

Before you leave, investigate the availability of internet, telephone and electricity so that you can remain connected while you travel.

How are the internet services in the host country?

_____

_____

_____

Is there internet available in my accommodation?

_____

_____

_____

What kind of telephone cards are available? Where do I buy them?

_____

_____

_____

What kind of electrical plugs do they have? Do I need an adapter?

_____

_____

What is the voltage? Are power outages common?

_____

_____

_____

Gear

Some specific gear may be required depending on your destination. Check if there are items which can make your travel easier.

Are there any special items to take along?

_____

_____

_____

Do I want to take a camera? Do I already have the one I want?

_____

_____

_____

Should I take a phone/computer/tablet?

_____

_____

_____

Do I need to bring any specific items (e.g., towels, bedding, etc.)?

_____

_____

_____

Backpack or suitcase?

_____

_____

Cash and Credit Cards

Look into how you will be able to get cash while you are travelling. Check what kind of fees your bank will charge for foreign withdrawls. Are ATMs easily accessible?

_____

_____

_____

What does my bank charge for international withdrawls?

_____

_____

_____

What type of credit cards are accepted most easily in the location?

_____

_____

_____

What are the charges for international transactions?

_____

_____

_____

Are there special credit card deals I can find to reduce the fees?

_____

_____

_____

Get ready for your volunteer project

Get information about where you will be living and working. It is helpful to try to understand what to expect.

What will I be doing in my project?

_____

_____

_____

_____

Do I need to get a background check?

_____

_____

Do I need to bring any materials for my project?

_____

_____

What is the dress code?

_____

_____

What are the working hours?

_____

_____

Will I be working alone or with other volunteers?

_____

Get ready for your volunteer project

What will my accommodations be like?

_____

_____

_____

_____

Are there things I need to bring along (bedding, towels, etc.)?

_____

_____

Are meals provided? If yes, which meals?

_____

_____

Is it easy to buy toiletries and over-the-counter medication locally?

_____

_____

Do I need to bring gifts (e.g., for my host family)?

_____

_____

Can my special dietary needs be met?

_____

Get ready for your volunteer project
Questions and Notes

_____

_____

_____

_____

_____

_____

_____

_____

_____

_____

_____

_____

_____

_____

_____

_____

_____

Get ready for your volunteer project
Setting Expectations

It is very important to be clear about your expectations for your volunteer project and the project's expectations for you. The more these are discussed upfront, the less chance for disappointment and problems during the course of the work. Be open in your communication, everyone wants the project to be a big success!

The project organizers will have expectations of you, such as being punctual and respecting the work schedule, communicating any issues, and maintaining confidentiality with sensitive information. Ask the project organizers to share their expectations of you to avoid any misunderstandings.

You should also be clear about what you expect from your project organizers. The following list has some suggestions for you to discuss with the project leaders.

- What are my work responsibilities?
- Will you introduce me to the people I will work with?
- What are the housing guidelines (if housing is provided)?
- How does the organization work?
- What is the protocol for handling any issues, concerns or complaints?
- How will you review and evaluate my performance?
- Will I incur any expenses for doing my project? Will they be reimbursed?
- Will I live at/near the place where I work?

Some of these discussions can happen before you travel and many of them will happen upon your arrival. Be sure to ask any questions and keep the lines of communication open throughout your project.

Every person can make a difference, and every person should try.

- John F. Kennedy

Funding

Your initial budget will tell you how much money you need for your trip. Now you have to determine how to fund your travel. There are many options depending on how long you will travel and the kind of volunteer work you will be doing.

If you have enough money for your travel, you can skip this step. Or, you may consider fundraising for your project (check with the local organization and/or your agency to discuss details).

You can fundraise to pay for your volunteer work or apply for scholarships. If you are planning a long trip, you can even consider selling some things or giving up/sub-leasing your apartment/ house. Ask friends and family for ideas and get creative!

On the next 2 pages, you can keep track of ideas and sources for money. On the pages after that, you can track the money you have made/saved for the trip.

Funding idea _____

_____

Estimated Funding _____

Action Steps

❏ _____

❏ _____

❏ _____

Funding idea _____

_____

Estimated Funding _____

Action Steps

❏ _____

❏ _____

❏ _____

Funding idea _____

_____

Estimated Funding _____

Action Steps

❏ _____

❏ _____

❏ _____

Funding idea _____

_____

Estimated Funding _____

Action Steps

☐ _____

☐ _____

☐ _____

Funding idea _____

_____

Estimated Funding _____

Action Steps

☐ _____

☐ _____

☐ _____

Funding idea _____

_____

Estimated Funding _____

Action Steps

☐ _____

☐ _____

☐ _____

Money available for travel

Source and date	Amount

Money available for travel

Source and date	Amount
_____	_____
_____	_____
_____	_____
_____	_____
_____	_____
_____	_____
_____	_____
_____	_____
_____	_____

My Funding Progress

0% (| | |) 100%

total amount needed _____

Volunteering is the ultimate exercise in democracy. You vote in elections once a year, but when you volunteer, you vote every day about the kind of community you want to live in.

- Author Unknown

Packing Lists

Most people suggest taking less rather than more on your travel abroad. This is good advice! Here are a few questions to help you decide what to take along.

- Can I have laundry done nearby?
- Do I need towels, bedding, sleeping bag, etc.? If yes, can I buy it nearby instead of taking it with me?
- For outdoor work, do I need work gloves, tools, etc.?
- Can I recharge my camera, phone, laptop, etc.? If electricity is limited, is there power for some hours each day or only a few hours a week?

Some essential items:

- A daypack to carry water, camera, etc.
- A small medical kit (see separate list).
- Toiletries (see separate list). Ask what you can find in the local shops. Consider taking extra contacts/glasses if you need them, since getting replacements can be difficult. Take lens solution if you use contact lenses.
- Copies of key documents such as travel information and your passport. Email them to yourself for easy access.

When you consider your clothing, think about items you can mix and match. You will probably need something nice, though it's unlikely you'll need formal clothing. For most projects, it is appropriate to dress conservatively, so save your shorts and tank tops for outside work hours. Ask your project coordinator about special requirements for your project.

On the next pages are basic lists to use as a start point. There are more detailed lists and resources at www.PlanToVolunteer.com. Add or remove items based on your project and the local climate. Above all, don't worry, you can buy a lot of items locally; these can make great souveniers!

Packing List

- [ ] Hat
- [ ] Hiking shoes
- [ ] Light rain jacket
- [ ] Long pants
- [ ] Long-sleeved shirts
- [ ] Sandals/flip flops
- [ ] Shorts
- [ ] Sneakers
- [ ] Socks / Underwear
- [ ] Sunglasses
- [ ] Swimming suit
- [ ] T-shirts (try wool!)
- [ ] Battery pack
- [ ] Books
- [ ] Camera
- [ ] Computer/tablet
- [ ] Electrical Adaptor
- [ ] Flashlight
- [ ] Small knife
- [ ] Ziploc bags

- [ ] _____
- [ ] _____
- [ ] _____
- [ ] _____
- [ ] _____
- [ ] _____
- [ ] _____
- [ ] _____
- [ ] _____
- [ ] _____
- [ ] _____
- [ ] _____
- [ ] _____
- [ ] _____
- [ ] _____
- [ ] _____
- [ ] _____
- [ ] _____
- [ ] _____
- [ ] _____

Packing List

- [ ] _____
- [ ] _____
- [ ] _____
- [ ] _____
- [ ] _____
- [ ] _____
- [ ] _____
- [ ] _____
- [ ] _____
- [ ] _____
- [ ] _____
- [ ] _____
- [ ] _____
- [ ] _____
- [ ] _____
- [ ] _____
- [ ] _____
- [ ] _____

- [ ] _____
- [ ] _____
- [ ] _____
- [ ] _____
- [ ] _____
- [ ] _____
- [ ] _____
- [ ] _____
- [ ] _____
- [ ] _____
- [ ] _____
- [ ] _____
- [ ] _____
- [ ] _____
- [ ] _____
- [ ] _____
- [ ] _____
- [ ] _____

Toiletries Packing List

- ☐ Toothbrush _____
- ☐ Toothpaste _____
- ☐ Shampoo _____
- ☐ Body soap _____
- ☐ Comb/brush _____
- ☐ Shaving gear _____
- ☐ Deodorant _____
- ☐ Travel towel _____
- ☐ Hand sanitizer _____
- ☐ Sunscreen _____

- ☐ _____
- ☐ _____
- ☐ _____
- ☐ _____
- ☐ _____
- ☐ _____
- ☐ _____
- ☐ _____
- ☐ _____
- ☐ _____

First Aid Packing List

- ☐ Band Aids _____
- ☐ Pain reliever _____
- ☐ Antidiarrheal _____
- ☐ Insect repellant _____
- ☐ Immunization card _____
- ☐ Anti-itch cream _____
- ☐ Antihistimines _____
- ☐ Lip Balm _____
- ☐ _____

- ☐ _____
- ☐ _____
- ☐ _____
- ☐ _____
- ☐ _____
- ☐ _____
- ☐ _____
- ☐ _____
- ☐ _____

Packing Notes

"Wherever you turn, you can find someone who needs you. Even if it is a little thing, do something for which there is no pay but the privilege of doing it. Remember, you don't live in a world all of your own."

- Albert Schweitzer

Go!
Enjoy Your Volunteer Project

On the Way
First Impressions
Journal
Observations on volunteer project

Volunteers are love in motion!

- Author Unknown

On the Way

Take a little time to reflect on the adventure in front of you. It will enhance your observation and experience.

What are 3 words to describe my host country?

_____

_____

_____

What do I imagine the location will be like?

_____

_____

_____

_____

_____

What do I think the people will be like?

_____

_____

_____

_____

_____

_____

What do I think it will be like in my volunteering project?

_____

_____

_____

_____

_____

_____

_____

What do I imagine I will do in my free time/travel time?

_____

_____

_____

_____

_____

_____

_____

First Impressions

Of the country/location

_____

_____

_____

_____

_____

_____

_____

_____

Of the host location/family

_____

_____

_____

_____

_____

_____

_____

_____

First Impressions

Of the project

_____

_____

_____

_____

_____

_____

_____

Other observations and thoughts

_____

_____

_____

_____

_____

_____

_____

Journal

You'll have new experiences every day to notice and record. Your journal will be a great way to remember even the smallest details long after they fade from your memory. Some days it is difficult to think about what to write. Below is a list of prompts to help you on those days.

* What are the biggest differences between where I am living now and my hometown?
* What is something interesting I noticed on my way to my project today?
* What is the funniest thing that happened this week?
* What is my favorite new food?
* What are 3 things I appreciate more about home?
* What is my favorite new word in a foreign language?
* What is the first thing I will do when I get home?
* What do I enjoy most about being abroad?
* What is the most challenging about being abroad?
* What 10 words describe how I am feeling today?
* One person I won't forget when I go home is...
* Three things that surprise me about living in _____
* What is something people do here which is different from home?
* List everything that happened today (this will be fun to read a year from now!).
* How am I different since I arrived?
* The next place I want to travel to is ....

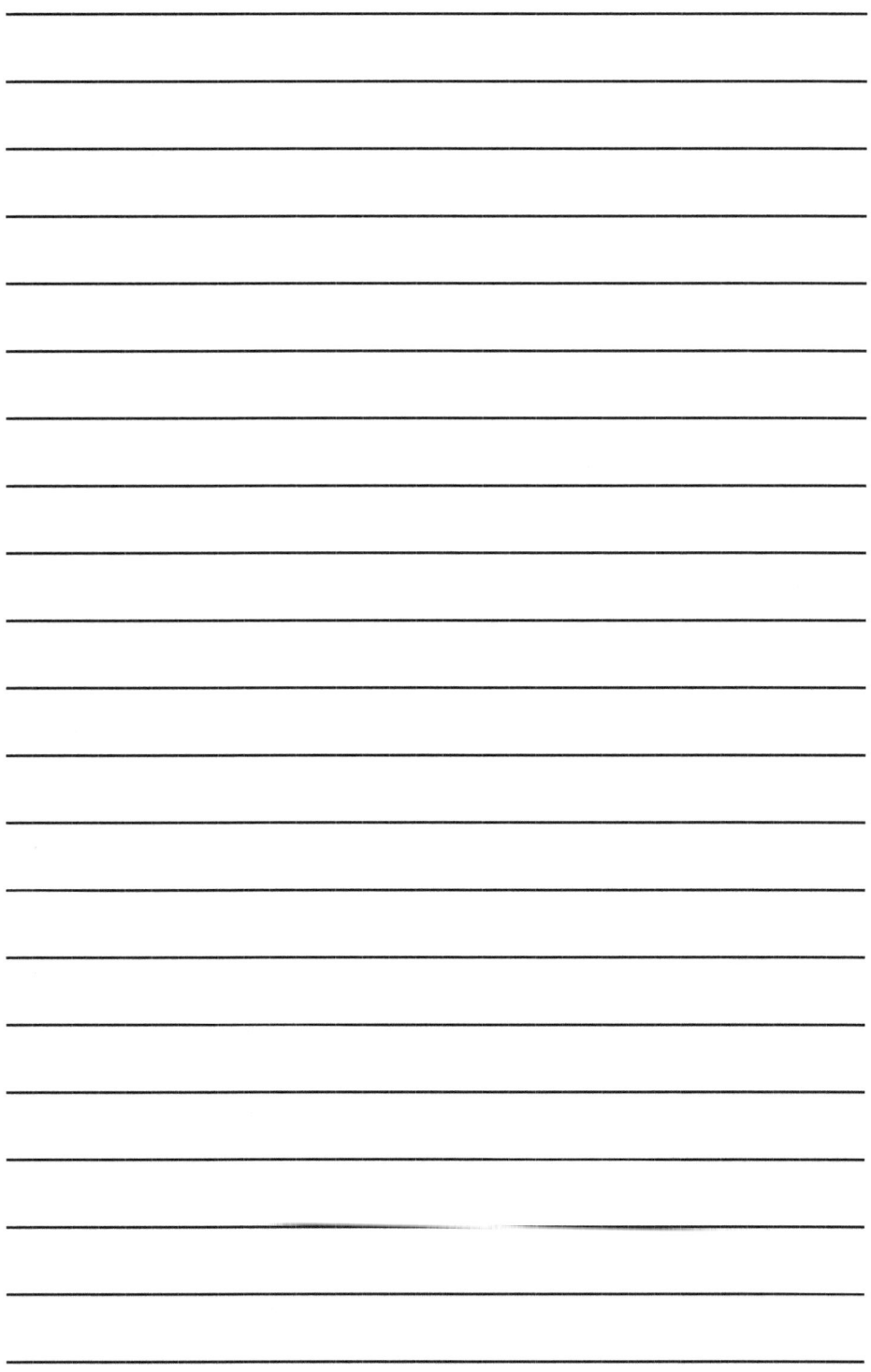

Observations on your Volunteer Project

At the end of your project, you will be asked to provide feedback on the project, location and organization. Take some notes along the way to be able to provide helpful, data based feedback and help the organization continue to improve.

What worked well at this project? _____

_____

_____

_____

_____

_____

_____

How could the project have been more effective or efficient?

_____

_____

_____

_____

_____

_____

_____

What did this organization do well? _____

_____

_____

_____

_____

_____

_____

_____

_____

How could this organization be more effective or efficient?

_____

_____

_____

_____

_____

_____

_____

_____

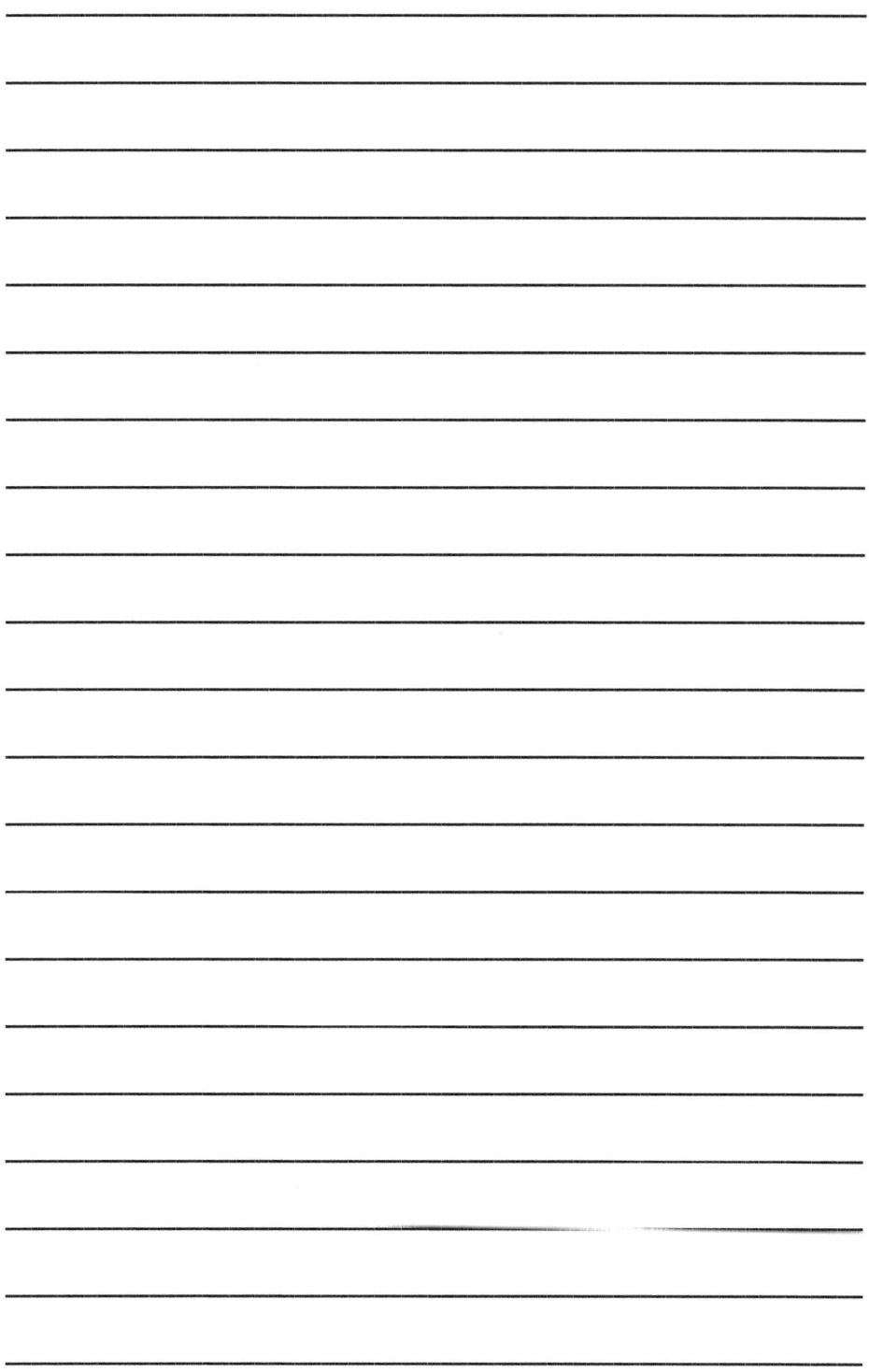

Reference & Tracking

Itinerary
Important Contacts
Expense Tracker

Wherever a man turns he can find someone who needs him.

- Albert Schweitzer

Itinerary

Date _____

From _____ To _____

Booking reference _____

Notes _____

_____

_____

Date _____

From _____ To _____

Booking reference _____

Notes _____

_____

_____

Date _____

From _____ To _____

Booking reference _____

Notes _____

_____

_____

Itinerary

Date _____

From _____ To _____

Booking reference _____

Notes _____

_____

_____

Date _____

From _____ To _____

Booking reference _____

Notes _____

_____

_____

Date _____

From _____ To _____

Booking reference _____

Notes _____

_____

_____

Itinerary

Date _____

From _____ To _____

Booking reference _____

Notes _____

_____

_____

Date _____

From _____ To _____

Booking reference _____

Notes _____

_____

_____

Date _____

From _____ To _____

Booking reference _____

Notes _____

_____

_____

Important Contacts & Phone Numbers

Doctor at home

Name: _____

Phone:_____ Email:_____

Credit card contacts in case of theft/loss

Company:_____ Phone: _____

Company:_____ Phone: _____

Company:_____ Phone: _____

Bank contacts

Contact: _____ Phone: _____

Contact: _____ Phone: _____

Insurance contact in case of emergency

Phone 1:_____ Phone 2: _____

Email: _____

Address:_____

Embassy

Phone:_____ Email:_____

Address: _____

Important Contacts & Phone Numbers

Volunteer agency

Contact: _____   Email:_____

Phone:_____

Accommodation address: _____

_____

Postal address: _____

_____

Project address: _____

Additional Contacts

Contact: _____   Email:_____

Phone:_____   Note:_____

Contact: _____   Email:_____

Phone:_____   Note:_____

Contact: _____   Email:_____

Phone:_____   Note:_____

Contact: _____   Email:_____

Phone:_____   Note:_____

Contact: _____   Email:_____

Phone:_____   Note:_____

The interior joy we feel when we have done a good deed is the nourishment the soul requires.

- Albert Schweitzer

Expense Tracker

Tracking your expenses will help you manage your budget as you travel. It will also help you keep track of your expenses as you prepare for your trip.

Item	Cost	Date/Location
flight		
visa		
passport		
volunteer registration		
volunteer program cost		

Expense Tracker

Item	Cost	Date/Location

Expense Tracker

Item	Cost	Date/Location

Expense Tracker

Item	Cost	Date/Location

Expense Tracker

Item	Cost	Date/Location

Expense Tracker

Item	Cost	Date/Location

Expense Tracker

Item	Cost	Date/Location

Expense Tracker

Item	Cost	Date/Location

Expense Tracker

Item	Cost	Date/Location

About the Author

Heidi van 't Riet was born in the USA and grew up in North Carolina. After she graduated from university, she started exploring the world. She moved to Europe where she completed an MBA in the Netherlands and Spain. Over the next 20 years, she lived in six different countries working for a Fortune 100 company.

After leaving corporate life, Heidi got involved in education and became the Chairman of the Board of an international school in Vienna, Austria. In 2014, she and her husband decided there was more to life than work, and they took their children on an 8-month trip around the world.

A substantial part of their voyage was dedicated to volunteering projects in Ecuador, Peru, Vietnam, Nepal, and Laos. This personal experience, combined with observing other volunteers and many interactions with volunteer agencies around the world became the basis of this practical (work-) book.

Heidi's passion for travel, care for people and the environment, as well as her skill set in management, allowed her to put together this useful tool for those seriously considering (but perhaps not fully sure how to) volunteer.

For more information, please visit www.PlanToVolunteer.com.

www.ingramcontent.com/pod-product-compliance
Lightning Source LLC
Chambersburg PA
CBHW072133020426
42334CB00018B/1781